The Oldest Rookie:
"Never Give Up"

by
Kelvin Davis

Kelvin Davis

256 690-9975¹

Kelvin Davis

ISBN-13: 978-0-578-81392-9

Printed in the U.S.A.

First Edition

Table of Contents

DEDICATIONS

I would like to dedicate this book to my uncle, Dr. Joseph "Joe" L. Reed.

Thank you for being a father figure to my siblings, my cousins, and I. It is with great joy that I dedicate this book to you, because you have instilled so many great things in us from childhood and as we grew. I would like to give a special thanks to Aunt Mollie for sharing you with us. Thank you for the fishing and hunting trips you took us on. You were always someone that we could look up to.

You were the spark that ignited the flame in us to be great at whatever we set out to do. I have watched you be a voice of freedom throughout the Civil Rights movement. You were the trailblazer that opened so many opportunities for others around us.

On behalf of myself and the eleven others, I dedicate this book to the greatest uncle in the world, Dr. Joseph L. Reed.

The Oldest Rookie "It's Never to Late!"

Pictured: Kelvin's Mom, Verba, Grandmother, Eula and Great-Grandmother, Nora

ACKNOWLEDGEMENTS

In Loving Memory of my wonderful mother Verba Davis. I say thanks for all that you instilled in me and my siblings. You were such an inspiration to me in so many ways. The memory of you will forever live in my heart, mind, body and soul. You were the greatest Mom that I could have ever had. Watching you raise four kids and seven more of our cousins was so amazing. I saw how you never gave up and now I apply those principles to my own life. You helped paved the way for me to make world history! I Love You Always.

To my father - I use to wonder where I got my zeal and drive from and I now realize that it came from you, Matthew Davis. You continue to amazement by speaking fluent Spanish and writing amazing books! Thank you for instilling a spirit of excellence and ambition. I love you. And Special Thanks to Barbra "Mama B" for being such a special person in all of our lives.

Special Thanks to my wife, Judie, who is a great inspiration to me in every endeavor. Your relentless strength and ability to impact others in such a phenomenal way is a gift that I cherish in you. Not only are you a great wife, you are my best friend. I appreciate your support to the utmost. I love you in a special way.

To my children who helped push me on this journey-Kendon, Terrance, Danielle, Kelvin, Princeton, and Samuel, you are the greatest!

Thanks to my siblings Terry, Deborah, Danny, Rodney, Carl and Lynn for putting up with your baby brother. You all were my balance in life. Without such great siblings around me, I could have had a negative outcome. But you all help me to develop into the person I am today. I'm forever indebted.

Special Thanks to all of my Brother-in-laws & Sister-in-laws for your love and support.

Special Thanks to my Aunt Ann, Uncle Brilly, Aunt Pat, Aunt Geraldine, Aunt Lillie Mae and to my cousins Larry and Jean for their unconditional support.

Thank you to my neighbors, Earl Evans and family.

I would like to thank my high school teammates: Arnold Coker, Jimmy Sumpter, Jaye Phillipi, Gabriel Maxwell, Donald Lampkins, Tim Roberson, and Larry Woods.

To my best friend Gary Gross, who taught me how to be tough mentally. To Raymond Bruce who taught me the importance of defense. To Larry Maxwell who taught me how to lead with confidence. Thank you to my high school coach Danny Covin who allowed me to be myself and to play my game. Thank you to my junior college team mates, Frank and John Williams and David "Jam" Washington.

I'd also like to give a special thanks to my college teammates. Clayton Harris, who taught me how to handle the basketball and how to be a floor general. He always had mad handles. To Kevin Loder who could shoot the lights out. He later went on to play basketball in the NBA. I learned so much from you, Kevin. I would like to say thanks to my head coach at Alabama State University, Coach James Oliver. First, you taught me to be a respectable young man. Secondly, you taught me how to be a great basketball player. The work ethic you instilled in me has brought me to this plateau. The 5 a.m. workouts and the two-a-day practices, made me mentally tough. I thank you with humble gratitude for the positive impact you have made in my life. Love you Coach.

I would like to Thank my friend, Bishop David Powel for all your Support and Inspiration.

Special Thanks to Ossie and Jessie Peacock for their faith to never give up in tough times. I also want to say a special thanks to my friends, Duane and Victoria Batiste.

I want to acknowledge and thank, Ebone Cambell for her outstanding work and performance as my representative and assistant in getting such great opportunities for my talent to be recognized.

I want to say thanks to the leaders that helped groom and teach me in the things of God: Bishop Ray Trout, Bishop Joel Trout, Bishop Franklin McNeil, Dr. Johnny Burrell and Assistant Pastor Reginald Burrell.

And lastly, Thank You to my Publishing Team who helped me birth this project:

My niece and Editor, Shaunda Davis Mathieu of His Write Hand Publishing powered by SDM Enterprises. Contact info: Email: adavismathieu@gmail.com Phone: (678) 200-3660

My Friend and brother, Apostle Larry D. Sims from KingdomSystic Publishing who formatted everything and assisted in the publishing process. Contact info: Email: Kingdomsystic@gmail.com Phone: (256) 345-8754

And to my Book Cover designer, Bobby Booker, Thank you for an AWESOME Job. Your design skills are second to none!

THE OLDEST ROOKIE: "NEVER GIVE UP"
BY: KELVIN DAVIS

INTRODUCTION

As a child I'd always dreamed of playing professional basketball. I grew up in a small town called Evergreen, Alabama. Born to the proud parents of Matthew and Verba Davis, I am the youngest of four children: Terry, Deborah, Carl and Yours Truly.

My passion for basketball started early when I was around 7 years old. I would go out to the old dirt court and shoot baskets alone. I would always pretend to be one of the NBA stars such as Jo Jo White, Kareem Abdual Jabbar or Earl the Pearl Monroe.

I would get the ball and start counting backwards "5,4,3,2,1..." and at the last second, I would hit the winning shot. I would yell to the top of my voice "HE MAKES IT!!!

Kelvin Davis just scored the winning basket with NO time left on the clock!". How exciting and motivational that was for me! It pushed me to continue pursuing my dream.

By the time I reached age ten, I started playing with guys that were older than me. They would pick me to play with them even though they were older, bigger, and stronger than me. Sometimes I got roughed up because the games were so physical. Little did I know that I was being made stronger, faster and smarter. As time went on, I was able to hold my own and compete with them with no problem. Now a buzz was going around the community about how I was developing into a great basketball player.

FIRST QUARTER

My First Tryout

I attended Lyeffion Middle and High School. I was so determined to make the team. I prepared and worked hard to make sure that I was going to make it. After tryouts I learned that I MADE THE TEAM!!! Back in my day, the Jerseys that we wore looked like white t-shirts. The number on the Jersey was handwritten with a black Magic Marker.

 However, don't let the homemade jersey-wearing team fool you. When we took the court, the opposing team was in for a real battle. My position was the Point Guard. All the plays came through me. I could feel my confidence growing when we would play other teams and I was able to score most of the time at will.

My next step was the High School Team. My senior year I averaged 21 points and 7 rebounds.

One of my greatest moments of playing high school basketball was "The County Tournament". This was when all the schools in the county would compete for a championship game in our area. We made it to the finals and were matched up with a school called the Evergreen Aggies. They were the Goliaths that were seemingly hard to defeat.

My school had not beat this team in 17 years. When the game started nobody gave us a chance. Everyone thought the game be would be a blow out.

The game started, and we were going neck to neck. The gym was packed, and the crowd was going wild. The highlight of the game was when one of their players who was about 6'4 stole the ball and was coming down court. I was the only man back to defend him. As he went up over the rim I met him in mid-air and BLOCKED his shot.

The crowd went WILD!!! We managed to defeat the Aggies on their home court 39 to 44. I scored 11 points and grabbed 16 rebounds. We had a major celebration that night!

College

After high school I decided to attend Junior College at Jefferson Davis Jr. College in Brewton, Alabama. I was invited to tryouts by Coach Cannon.

Coach Cannon approached me after tryouts and said "I like your game. I want to offer you a scholarship to play at our college." I accepted. I was the Point Guard and we came very close to winning the JUCO State Tournament. We lost by a few points in the semi-finals to Lawson State (I detest losing).

After JUCO I was recruited by Alabama State University in Montgomery Alabama. I signed with them in 1979. We had an awesome team!

Pictured: College Team Mates, Frank Williams and John Williams.

Our regular season record was 27-1. We were ranked number 1 in the nation. I remember one game. We were playing a school called the University of Alabama at Huntsville. They had a Point Guard that was shooting the lights out-no one could stop him.

Coach Oliver looked down the bench and said "Davis, get in the game and I want you to stop that guy from scoring". When the crowd saw me get up, they started cheering and clapping. Defense was my specialty. It was about 10 minutes left in the half. I shut him down! He didn't score another point for the entire half!

Junior College Experience

Jefferson Davis State Junior College, now known as CACC. I would like to say that I am very grateful for my junior college coach, Frank Cannon. I was invited by him to come and try out with his team.

During the tryouts, my game was spot on. I had a tremendous leaping ability and slam dunk with authority. When the try out was over, coach came over to me and told me that he wanted to offer me a scholarship at that very moment to play for the school.

I told him that I would have to talk it over with my mother first and he let me know that that would be fine. I later spoke with my mother and she thought that it was a great idea! I signed for the scholarship and began attending CACC.

Coach Cannon saw something special in me that day. He saw what I could be in the future for this team. We had a great team and we made it to the second round of the Junior College tournament.

We had a set of twins on the team, Frank and John Williams. Frank was a strong power forward and John was a pure shooter. I was the point guard and had to make sure the ball was distributed to the right person and get the ball where it needed to go.

One night we were playing in the tournament and John was shooting the lights out. I dribbled the ball down the court and coach yelled for me to give the ball to John. "He is hot!" he yelled.

This was a great learning experience for me. When another player is on a roll, you must let them roll. I had to learn the strength of my players. One of my teammates, David "Jam" Washington, could run the floor and could catch the ball off the wing and thrust it down with power.

Basketball is a fast pace game and you must make quick decisions within seconds. The word of God says to know those who labor among you. Whether it's a work, church, or on a team, it's good to know who has what strengths and abilities. By this, you know how to delegate your authority. Again, I would like to thank all my JUCO teammates for trusting me to be their floor general.

After College

I moved to Huntsville, Alabama where I was a Physical

Education Teacher. I got a second job working on the campus at Alabama A&M University as a Residence Hall Manager. One day the basketball team was running some pick-up games. I asked them if I could get in the next game. They reluctantly said yes. Well, when the game was over, they were all looking at me in amazement saying, "WOW, where did this guy come from?!?". I competed with them when they thought it would be a walk in the park. My team won the game. From that point on I had their respect and they always wanted me to play with them every time I came in the gym. Never judge a person by their age.

Pictured: Kelvin's Son Prince, Daughter-in-law Jada, Daughter Danielle, Son Kendon and Son Terrance.

My Move to Atlanta, Georgia

I'd always wanted to move to Atlanta and one day the opportunity presented itself. My children didn't want to leave Decatur, AL but I thought it would be a great change. Relocating my entire family proved to be more challenging that I'd anticipated. Our first major hurdle was finding a house. We looked at dozens of houses in different neighborhoods and finally I spotted a home I thought would be the perfect fit for our family. As soon as the realtor opened the door to the home, we knew that this was it. Now it was time to check out the school system. I did some research and to my surprise, Fayette County was one of the top school systems in the state of Georgia. What a relief! I rented a U-Haul with a trailer and off we went to start a new life in Atlanta, GA.

After getting settled, I found a local gym where I could continue shooting hoops. These guys were exceptional players. One day as I was playing, some Pro players approached me and asked how old I was. When I replied 46 years old, they couldn't believe it. They said, "Do you know you can play professional ball right now with your skills?" I was thrilled that they thought so much of my game. I told them I am going to do just that and tryout with a professional team.

Kelvin's Wife, Judie and his youngest son, Samuel

Pictured: Kelvin's Son, Princeton Slam Dunking. He Got Hops!!

One night while attending an Atlanta Hawks game, I saw Dennis Scott (formerly of the Orlando Magic) talking to another tall gentleman. When they finished talking, the gentleman walked right pass me. I stopped him and said "Sir, do you play pro ball?". He said "No, I own the new professional basketball team here in Atlanta." I told him that I knew someone that wanted to try out for his team. He gave me his card and said, "Tell them to give me a call."

Kelvin with his family along with NBA Great, Kevin Johnson @ Lolos Restaurant.

Well, little did he know that I was the one that wanted to tryout. Yes, me-the 47-year old guy. After a few days went by, the owner called and said "Sir, this is Quentin Townsend. You remember I met you at the Atlanta Hawks game and told me that you knew someone that wanted to try out for my team? Who is it?" I said "Me". He immediately started laughing and replied, "*You* want to try out with my team?" I said "Yes, I can run with your guys." He responded with "I will call you later".

One week went by and there was no call. The second week my phone rang He said "Hello Kelvin, this is the Owner of The Atlanta Vision. I want to see you play. My team will be working out Monday at 9:00am-be there." I responded, "Yes Sir!". I was excited about the opportunity. Wow!!! My mind was running 100 miles per hour in excitement.

When I got there, I got loose and warmed up my 47-year old legs. When we started to play, my jumper was wet with sweat. I was crashing the boards and snatching rebounds over guys twice my size. I could see the expression on Mr. Townsend's face as I was playing. His mouth and his eyes were wide open. His players couldn't believe what had just happened. They were just as amazed as he was.

After workouts were over, he called me over to the bleachers where he was sitting, looking astonished and bewildered. He said "Kelvin, you've exceeded all my expectations! I want you to come and tryout with my team." He said, "Run five miles a day and eat plenty of bananas!"

Well I took his advice, hitting those five miles and eating bananas every day. I also lifted weights and did as many sit-ups and pushups as I could handle. I could feel myself getting stronger and stronger. I believe in being prepared for every opportunity-especially now that I had an opportunity to fulfil my lifelong dream!

To make sure my shooting eye was right, I had trainer Max Mullin to assist me. His nickname was MAD MAX. Thankfully, he pushed me to my limits, and I came to understand exactly how he got his nickname. I would be extremely sore after workouts, but I was determined that I wouldn't let anything stop me. I want to encourage you to NEVER give up on your dreams-no matter how hard life gets.

Eating to Win

It's true-you are what you eat. Whatever you put in your body has a direct effect on you. I had to eat balanced meals that included fruits and vegetables. I had to avoid excess sugar like the plague. I would start my day off with water. Water is so vital to the body. For adult men, about 60 percent of their bodies is water; for females, 55 percent is made of water. It's crucial to replenish your body with what you are made of-WATER.

I would start my day by eating two bananas for breakfast, followed by oatmeal for fiber and eggs for my protein. For lunch I would do a Chick-Fila Southwest Grilled Salad, which I grew to love. Eating fresh salads helps to assist  the digestive process and provides nutrients. To perform at a high level of professional basketball, I could not afford to be sluggish. A healthy diet enabled me to outlast and out-perform players 27 years younger than me, so remember to EAT HEALTHY!

SECOND QUARTER

Prepping for the Pros

I knew I had to be prepared for the challenge and chance of a lifetime. After all, how many guys get recruited to try out for a professional basketball team at the age of 47 years old? The first thing I would do every morning is acknowledge God and thank Him for giving me this opportunity. Then it was workout time.

1. Stretch very well before engaging in running.

2. 5 mile run nonstop.

3. Wind Sprints 50 dash 7 times

4. 25 push ups

5. 25 sit ups

6. Weights: curls 35 pounds 12 reps set of 3 7. Bench Press: 135 pounds 3 reps set of 3

Now this routine was just for off- court workouts. Many days I would go to the basketball court after my workout and sharpen my skills. My trainer would have me to put up hundreds of shots from all over the court to perfect my shot. I would do different types of footwork and dribbling drills to increase my ball handling skills. I would run several pick-up games to get my legs under me.

I cannot stress enough the importance of endurance. Stamina is a MUST when competing at this level. Either you prepare and succeed or you half step and fail. For me failure is not an option. I heard Kobe Bryant say his ability to outlast the opponents came from running sprints. I took his advice in preparing for the tryouts. After running a few miles, I would go to the gym and sprint over and over and over again. Let's face it-I would be competing against 19 and 20-year old youngsters, all of which I was old enough to be their father.

The Tryouts

As you can imagine, all kind of thoughts were running through my mind. When I walked in the gym everyone was looking at me like 'what is this guy doing here?'. The Tryouts were being conducted by NBA great Dennis Scott, formerly of the Orlando Magic. First, they stretched us and warmed us up very well because the next 2 days would be rigorous on the body. Drills started one after another. It was fast paced and intense. They were watching me to see if I would be able to endure this kind of regiment. Well it wasn't me that started giving up. Some of the young guys started to wear down quickly with fatigue. I could see it on their faces and in their body language. Some just stopped and walked off the court and gave up, but not me- my preparation paid off!

After drills they divided us into teams and had us scrimmage. We started playing and it was up and down... guys were dunking and shooting the rock like they were already in the pros. I wasn't going to let any of that intimidate me. I started shooting and the crowd went wild with cheers! I could tell the crowd was impressed by my skills and hearing them cheer only gave me more ammunition! I couldn't believe everyone was cheering for the 47-year old rookie!

Tryout Highlights

We had the ball and one of our guys shot and missed. I came in and leaped over everyone and grabbed the rebound. I threw it to one of our players, he shot and missed, I jumped over everyone again and got the rebound. The crowd started to go crazy!! I passed the ball to another player and he shot and missed it. I leaped over again and grabbed the rebound and pulled it down with authority.

The gym erupted with a loud shout. Dennis Scott was running up and down the sideline screaming and celebrating and yelling my name "KELVIN, YOU ARE SOMETHING ELSE!". The owner was just in awe of my hustle and determination. This goes to show that when you apply yourself that God will present a window of opportunity for you to shine above all the others you are competing against. What a moment to remember!

The Results

After tryout were over, the coaching staff and owners had us to sit down on the court. They congratulated everyone and said they would inform us by email of who is invited to Training Camp.

As you can imagine, I was pacing back and forth for days waiting to hear from the team to see if I was invited to Training Camp. It felt like the longest two days of my life. Finally, I got anxious and called the owner, Mr. Townsend. I said "Sir, have you all made a decision yet?". He insisted I had to wait and look at my email the next day. He told me that only 16 players would be invited to training camp.

Finally, the next day came and I pulled up the screen on my computer, opened my emailed, and looked at the list of names. One of them was MINE! I started screaming "I MADE IT!!!! I MADE IT!!!". The next thing I remember is my family jumping up and down and screaming to the top of their lungs. Things started to fall off the walls because of the vibrations from the celebration! What an amazing moment I was able to share with them!

The media quickly got wind that the 47-year old rookie was invited to camp. My phone started to ring off the hook from reporters asking me to do television interviews. I did one interview after another. Some came to my house and interviewed me, and others asked me to meet them at the gym. I was becoming a local celebrity!

Going the Extra Mile

When I say "Going the Extra Mile" I am referring to doing something above and beyond the ordinary. The first day of Training Camp the coaches ran us so hard you would think we were already in mid-season. Everybody was tired we were down to our last drill. Guys were leaning over with their hands on their knees, sweating and gasping for air. When the Coach finally dismissed us, everyone was so relieved. However, I sprinted down the floor to the other end and sprinted back while sweating and gasping for air.

Everyone was astonished including the owners and coaches. You could almost hear a pin drop! There are times when you'll have to push yourself beyond boundaries and self- limitation. Whatever your passion is, you must go after it with everything you have-might and soul. Nothing will come easy in life, but you must be proactive in your pursuit of your Dreams. Hurdles were put on the racetrack to be jumped over.

Obstacle are like hurdles -you must jump over them. Many times, you may be going through some personal situations at home or on the job. This is not a reason to quit or give up. This is where your greatness is revealed-when you are challenged in different areas of your life. When you overcome one thing, it encourages you to move keep moving towards your destiny. So, go the extra mile! DESTINY awaits you!

First Game, First Points

There were only a few minutes left in the game and I noticed my children sitting in the stands. I motion to them like I was eating with a fork to let them know I was hungry and that we were going to get something to eat after the game. That's when I heard the Coach yell "KELVIN, LETS GO MAN! GO CHECK IN THE GAME!".

Pictured:
Kelvin with former team mate, Coach Lewis Jackson

When I went to the score table everybody was yelling "Old School!!! Old School!!!". Even the opposing team was staring at me wondering if this was this true. Well as soon as I ran down the floor, the point guard passes me the ball in the corner. The guy guarding me got in his defensive stance to check me.

I blew right pass him went towards the basket, while his center who was 6'9 came over to prevent me from going to the basket. I leaped up towards the rim and he came hard to block my shot. I pulled the ball back and he fouled me very hard. I went to the free throw line and all eyes were on me. It was high pressure. The Referee gave me the ball and said, "Two shots!". Cameras were flashing, and the crowd was staring. I let the first shot

Credit: Commentator Dee Jackson

go and it was a SWISH. I shot the second one and it was a SWISH. After the game, the press came and interviewed me. The reporter asked me who were you talking to in the stands before the game. I explained that they were my children. I told the reporter that I was hungry at the time, but that all my hunger pains left as soon as the Coach called me into the game. The next day they wrote a major story on the entire night.

I also grabbed 3 rebounds in that game in a matter of 2:38 seconds. I felt like God had saved the best for last!! Sometimes our BEST days are just ahead of us, but we'll never get to see them if we give up too soon! Who would have thought that the game would end with ME making free-throws?! I strongly encourage you to go after your dreams with reckless abandon! The free-throws of your life are waiting to be shot, but only YOU can shoot them!

The Half-Court Shot

We were playing a game in Atlanta and with about 10 seconds on the clock, Coach called for me to get in the game. The other team had the ball. Well they thought they would throw a pass over my head to the guy I was guarding. But when they attempted to pass the ball over my head, the guy missed it. The ball went in the corner and I chased it down, grabbed it and started dribbling down court.

As soon as I crossed half- court, I shot a long shot and I made it! As the shot landed in the basket, the buzzer went off and the game was over. The gym exploded and people were running out on the floor like I had made a million-dollar shot. Well, to be honest, it felt like I had. My teammates were going crazy along with the coaches. That night, people rushed to take pictures with me and ask for my autograph. This was a night I'll never forget.

The Power of Positivity

Sometimes in life there will be times when it looks like all odds are against you. These are the times when you must keep a positive attitude and keep believing for the best outcome. I remember when I first set out to accomplish my dream as a pro ball player, people constantly reminded me of my age, saying "You're too old for that You can't keep up with those young guys". I had to reach way down in myself and ignore their comments because I knew in my heart that if I trained well and prepare myself, I would succeed.

Surround yourself with wholesome and healthy-minded people who speak the same language as you or better. I enjoy being around someone who knows more than me so I can glean from them and grow. Never be intimidated by people who are wiser or more intellectual or articulate than you are. Iron sharpens iron.

 When I play pick-up games with other players, I want to guard the best player on the opposing team. Why? Because he is going to bring out the best in my defensive skills which preparing me for the next tough guy I compete against.

Some of my favorite people to listen to are Dr. Bill Winston, an influential Pastor and leader in his community; Dr. Leo Lewis, An Apostolic Trailblazer & Prayer Warrior, Kobe Bryant, NBA Player. These are the people that I allow to speak into my life. Guard the "gates" to your inner being-what you see, hear, speak. Don't let anyone speak negativity, death, or defeat over your life.

I am grateful and thankful for Collin Millar and the All Nations Europe Prayer Team for their prayers. Also, to my mother-in-law, Mother Calie Gandy, who also covers us in prayer.

THIRD QUARTER

The NBA Calls

After two seasons with the American Basketball Association (ABA), they invited me back for a third season, but I declined because at this time, I was about to tum 50 years old. I had accomplished my purpose by becoming the Oldest Rookie.

Now the NBA had heard about me. I had my agent to give my information to the NBA Developmental League. The next thing I know I received a phone call from them. When I answered, the gentlemen said "Is this Kelvin Davis? We have selected you to come and participate in our Pre-Draft Camp in Los Angeles, California. Can you be there in July?", I replied "Yes Sir!". He said he would email me the dates and time.

MAN! My mind was running 101 miles per hour. I got on the phone and started telling my family about this awesome news. The next thing I know the television cameras were everywhere. I was being contacted by several television stations asking for interviews.

Preparation for Camp

After the dust had settled, it was back to the gym for workouts. I would get up in the morning and run between 5 and 7 miles. After running I would do sprints and weightlifting was also part of my training. I was now ready to go! I boarded my favorite Airline (Delta) and off to California I went!

When I arrived at the hotel, I saw so many tall and fit players that I was going to be playing against. But I didn't let that discourage me because I knew that my heart was just as BIG as they were TALL. They gave us a copy of the Itinerary. The first thing they wanted us to do was to attend an opening ceremony where we would be introduced and placed on the teams we would be playing.

The room was quite intimidating. It was huge and full of players, coaches and scouts. Next, they begin introducing each individual player. When they got to my name I stood up and walked toward the podium. I could hear whispers and chatter with a buzz going around the room. All eyes were on me, as if they were trying to decide if I were a coach or a player. They finally realized that I was a player and there to try-out for the NBA at 50 years old. They assigned me to the team that I would be playing with for the next 2 days. We boarded a huge charter bus and traveled to the Arena.

When we got off the bus, there were two players walking behind me talking. I heard one guy say to the other, "What is this guy doing here? Is he going to try and play against us?". They started to chuckle and tell jokes. I turned around, looked at them both and said, "I hope you brought you A-game!". I could tell that they were shocked at my response.

The NBA Tryouts

Now it was time to perform. They had us to do different stretches to get our body loose. This took around 25 minutes. Next, they had us to scrimmage against opposing teams. I started out banging it in the low post with the big guys. I grabbed several rebounds and was playing mad defense. The games were very competitive. I was just getting loose after the first 10 minutes. The young guys found out very quickly that I could keep up with them.

They were so surprised. Since this was a pre-draft camp, there were several NBA Scouts and D-League Coaches watching and taking notes. I was scoring baskets and rebounding with authority. During the game one of the guys accidently hit me across the face.

I just shook it off and kept playing. The next thing I know the Referee stopped the game and said "Sir, you are bleeding over your eye". I put my hand over my eye and blood was coming out of it. They sent me to the Training Room to see if they could close the cut. Thank God they were able to close it and put a patch over my eyebrow.

I went back to the bench and told the coach I wanted to go back in the game. They were surprised that I didn't sit it out and call it a day. If you are going to be great in life you can't let situations that are sometimes hard to stop your progress. I played even better after the injury.

I remember getting tangled up with the ball and the opposing player grabbed it. It turned out to be a jump ball. This guy was much taller than me, but when the Referee tossed the ball up, I outjumped him and everybody started cheering with amazement!

After Scrimmages, the younger players had a whole new perspective about the 50-year old player. When I got back to the hotel, they were storming me with questions, "How are you able to do all this at your age?". I told them that I'd worked hard to prepare myself for this challenge. I let them know that I didn't just come out and start playing, but that there was some blood, sweat and tears that went into getting me to this point. I let them know that nothing comes easy and that you can't let your feelings dictate your motivation.

Emotions fluctuate, but life goes on no matter how you feel. We must rise above feelings and conquer our fears.

The next day of workouts I had gotten a feel of the pace of the games. I played hard and I could see the Coaches and Scouts look at me in amazement. After the workouts were over, I thought they would tell us something about how we did. Instead, they said "We will let you know *if* we are interested in you". I said to myself "Kelvin, you gave it your best shot". I got on the plane and headed back to Atlanta for home.

The Phone Rang

I heard my cell phone go off and it was one of the Coaches from the Dallas Mavericks-League Team. He said, "May I speak to Kelvin?", I said "This is Kelvin". He said, "This is the Coach from the Dallas Mavericks. I saw you play the other day and I was very impressed with your hustle and the way you played.

He said I saw you when you got cut over your eye. I was watching to see if you would give it another try or sit it out. But when you returned to the game, I was impressed and that really caught my eye". He went on to invite me to come to Dallas and tryout with his team. I calmly thanked him for the opportunity, but inside I was exploding with joy.

I kept thinking "Wow!" I was sooo excited! News got out and the next thing I know there were TV cameras coming and people calling, wanting to set up interviews. Everyone wanted to meet the 51-year old that's trying out for the NBA. NEVER give up on your dreams!

FOURTH QUARTER

House Fire!!!

It was the night of Christmas Eve and my family and I had just returned from Birmingham, Alabama. We were all tired from the trip. Everyone else went upstairs to go to bed, but my youngest son Princeton and I sat down on the sofa. Soon, we were both fast asleep.

It was after midnight when I smelled a strange odor coming from somewhere. I took my son upstairs and put him in the bed with his mom. I told her that I smelled smoke coming from somewhere and I was going to check it out. I looked at the sofa and lifted it up. Underneath one of the cushions I saw something red that looked like hot charcoals. Next, I moved the sofa from the wall and immediately it burst into flames.

Frantically, I ran upstairs and woke up my wife. I yelled "The house is on fire!". She grabbed our son and went to the other room where my daughter and youngest son were sleeping. I could hear her yelling "Wake up! Wake up! The house is on fire!".

It was very cold outside, but we knew we had to get them out of the house because smoke was filling every room. After we got the children out, I went back inside to see if I could throw some water on the fire. The more water I threw, the larger the flames grew.

In a panic, I grabbed the burning couch and tried to drag it outside, but the flames were getting too large. I eventually had to drop the burning couch and just run for my life!

In our back yard was our big white German Shepherd. He was barking at the flames and running around like a wild animal. It was a challenge to get him out of the yard.

Finally, I got him and took him to the front yard where my family was standing in the cold with no shoes on. Now all the neighbors were out in the street, watching our home go up in flames. Our neighbors brought some blankets to shield the kids from the cold.

I could hear sirens in the background. The fireman got there and started to fight the blaze. By the time they were done it was a disaster. We lost everything in that fire...everything EXCEPT my faith!

Overcoming Obstacles

Now, as a father and head of the house, I had to rise to the occasion. To see my family standing outside in the cold bare feet, wrapped in blankets brought a feeling upon me that I will never forget. My first instinct was to be strong for my family but looking at them made me want to cry. I knew that I had to keep the family strong. The love and support poured in from our family and friends. Our insurance company got us a suite at the Residence Inn for several months.

So many people came and spent Christmas Day at the hotel with us. To get their minds off things, I would take the family on outings just to have fun. I wanted to give them something else to focus on besides our situation.

God gave me the strength and courage to step up to the plate and recover all that we'd lost. My advice to those reading this book is to NEVER quit because you never know when things can turn in your favor. I use this life experience when I am on the court. Be strong in the face of adversity. Opposition makes you stronger!!!

I want to encourage all those who have BIG dreams to keep those dreams alive. You were born to succeed. God wants you to succeed. You were born with certain gifts and qualities that are unique within themselves.

You can't let people or situations keep you from stepping out on nothing but believing that something is there. You must believe in yourself and not doubt. Just think about it, if you don't rise above fear and anxiety, you can't do that what seems impossible. All things are possible if you believe.

One day I was working out with my trainer and he informed me that he was inviting another trainer that he thought could help me out. I said "Okay, great. Let's do it". When he got there, we started working out and he asked me "Do you know what you are trying to do?". I said "Yes, why?". He said, "You are going to be playing against guys half your age". I told him that I'm not looking at their ages, but I'm looking at what I know is in my heart to do. I went and found my trainer. I told him that I never wanted to work with that guy again.

People tend to size you up with what is normal. Never allow anyone to put in in their category. You could be the next president of the United States or the very person to come up with a cure for cancer or some other type of disease.

You are not a regular Joe or Sue. You have greatness inside of you. Allow your mind to bring out the creativity in you-to bring forth your greatness. Never think small of yourself or your ideas. I realize this is a gift for me to be able to compete with young players in the game of Basketball, so I capitalized on my gift and my strengths thus making history as *the oldest rookie in the world to make the team*!

Even in a marriage, the Husband has strengths and the Wife has strengths. Let's say if the wife handles the finances better than the husband then she should be allowed to handle it. When you can delegate responsibility that takes pressure off you.

I think of it as ONE team striving for one common goal. When I am playing the game of basketball, I observe my teammates' strengths and weaknesses. If another guard can get the ball up the floor quicker than me, guess what? I'm going to get it in his hands and let him bring the ball up the floor.

In the meantime, I'm positioning myself to shoot a jumper. This is what makes great players great. They utilize their teammates to their advantage and do whatever it takes for the entire team to win.

Pictured: Kelvin's Mentor, Larry Maxwell, Pearl, Leslie and Kelvin

OVERTIME

From the Cotton Field to the Court

I remember growing up in the small town of Evergreen, Alabama. My mom would wake us up around 6:00 a.m. to go to the cotton fields to pick cotton. A man by the name of Mr. Johnson would pull into our yard and honk his horn.

My brothers and I would run out, hop on the back of the already crowded truck full of people, and we would try to find a space to sit. Many times, we would have to sit on top of each other. We would pick cotton all day long and at the end of the day, Mr. Johnson would weigh our sack full cotton, and would pay us five cents per pound. If you picked fifty pounds, you would get $2.50 for the day.

After working in the heat all day, we would all get back onto the packed truck and go back home. We worked for little of nothing.

People ask me why I play basketball with so much energy and intensity. I honestly believe that by being raised in such an unfair system, I would always tell them that whatever I do, I'm going to do it with all of my might.

When I was younger, I remember when it was time for the family to eat, the kids would have to stand and eat, because there was no room at the table. My mom raised her four children, along with some of my cousins.

Pictured: Kelvin's Family

In the 1960's there was also a lot of racism. I remember going to the movies and having to go to the side of the building to pay for my ticket, as opposed to going to the front of the theatre where all of the whites would enter. Once at the movies, I even remember having cold ice thrown on me.

I remember when the school bus would pick us up for school, that we would have to sit on the opposite side of the bus, from the whites because we were not allowed to sit together. These times were very tense and trying for the black community.

In 1968, I remember the shocking announcement from my teacher that Dr. Martin Luther King had been assassinated. I remember it just like it was yesterday. Through these tough times, basketball was my outlet and my get away to release any tension and frustrations of mine.

Through basketball, I was able to use it as a positive force that would change my entire life. Now, I'm able to look back at my life and see how I've gone from the cotton field to the court, to CNN, FOX, ABC and NBC, and to the World History Book. All I can say is Thank You Jesus!

Romans 8:28 says, "All things work together for the good of those who love God, to them who are the called according to His purpose. 1 Thessalonians 5:18 says, "In everything give thanks; for this is the will of God concerning you.

I am thankful for God placing the gift of playing basketball in me. He could have chosen someone else, but he chose me. Showing thanks is an expression of gratitude. When a child shows his parents that they are grateful for all their parents do for them. When this happens, the parents are more prone to do something even greater. Psalms 34:1 says, "I will bless the Lord at all times and His praise shall continually be in my mouth." I like how the word of God continually repeats this to me. Repeatedly notice how the scripture says, "at all times". This means that I will bless His name whether I have good or bad moments!

The Whooping of a Lifetime

One night my buddy and I went out to have some fun. His name was Greene Gross. Greene had a car and he stopped by to pick me up. As the night went on, we were having so much fun, not realizing the hour was getting later and later. Before I knew it, it was five in the morning. My plan was to quietly climb into my window.

So, I opened my window and jumped in. The next thing I knew, my mom was hitting me with a stick across my back! My mom had been waiting on me to come in and gave me a whooping that I will never forget.

Now, it didn't feel good, but now I can say that I appreciate her for chastising me with that whooping. It let me know that there are consequences to doing wrong, my mom was my greatest fan and her correction instilled discipline into my life. This also helped me on the court. Some things may not feel good, but it's for your good.

A man's gift makes room for him and bringeth him before great men. There is a song that says what God has for me, it is for me. God will position you where you need to be for your destiny. Your gift will open doors for you. It must be exposed to those who are waiting to hear your story. It must go forward! God has an audience that is tailor made specifically for your gifts.

I decree and declare that this year will be a year of open doors for you and that your dreams will come to pass. I pronounce a supernatural breakthrough for you, and that your vision and purpose to come forth in Jesus' name. Opportunity upon opportunity to come to you! Nothing can stop it nothing can block it. No demon can penetrate it. It will come forth now, by the authority of the kingdom of Heaven!

Facing Challenges

Challenges must be handled head on. First, we must recognize the challenge. People have challenges in different areas of their lives. Physical, Mental, Marriage, Divorce, Financial or whatever. Some situations come to test and try our very existence. Sometimes you just feel like giving up because the odds seem so insurmountable.

Remind yourself that you are not alone in your struggle. Look for any sources of help or hope. When I made the decision to try out for a Pro Team at age 47, I acknowledged that I would need some help.

My first step was to acknowledge God and to know that I couldn't do it without his help. Next, I hired a personal trainer. We call him Mad Max. I am saying this because many times we try to face our challenges alone but believe me, it's better to have help than trying to do it alone.

I view challenges like exercises. The more you work out, the stronger you get. I'm not saying that it's easy to conquer your giants but if you defeat your giants you get stronger. In some of our battles there are emotional and even sometimes physical scars inflicted on us. But whatever the residue is we can come out victorious.

No doubt life has a way of teaching us some tough lessons, but we must use these lessons as steppingstones to greater levels of opportunity. Don't be afraid to step up to the plate and knock a homerun! Someone is waiting to hear your story and you are the only one that can tell it.

COVID-19 Defeated

While at work one afternoon, I suddenly started to feel my body break out into a sweat. So much so, that I had to take off my shirt in order to cooldown.

I went to inform my supervisor about what was going on and let him know that I was not feeling very well. He then advised me to go to the doctor to get myself checked out.

I took his advice, clocked out, and headed to my car. At this point, I became overwhelmingly fatigued and my energy felt as if it was zapped from my body.

I drove myself to Piedmont Fayette Hospital's emergency room where the nurse checked all of my vital signs and drew my blood.

By now, I was experiencing chills and beginning to shake. The doctor then came in to examine me. He told me that I may have a cold or a small virus working its way through my system.

I asked him if they could test me for the COVID-19 virus and he told me no, since there were not enough symptoms. I was so disappointed that he would not give me the test. He told me to take some Tylenol and to self-quarantine myself for fourteen days.

Even then, I realized that I couldn't be around my family because I was so unsure of the extent of my sickness. After all of this was completed, I called my uncle who takes care of our family home in Montgomery, Alabama. He told me to come and to stay as long I needed to heal and recover.

First Fourteen Days of Quarantine

The first day of my quarantine I was still very fatigued. I began to cough, and my appetite was surely fading. After a while of feeling this way, I called my brother and sister-in-law to let them know how I was feeling. My sister-in-law had a nurse to call me so that I could let her know about my symptoms as well.

Once I told the nurse how I was feeling, she asked if I wanted to be tested for the COVID-19 virus, and I told her yes! I scheduled an appointment and was tested the following day.

The test was the most painful and uncomfortable thing that I've ever felt! It felt as if someone had taken burning match and pushed it up my nose. The results came back positive for the virus. Wow! What a shocker!

Even in this, I knew that I now had to use some of the same skills that I would normally use in basketball. I had to dig deep within myself and put my trust and confidence in my God. During my illness I began to understand the importance of family. My wife was so supportive and encouraging. Since I was quarantined away from home, we would Facetime each other almost all day long. My siblings, children, aunts and uncles, cousins, nieces, and ministry friends were all so supportive. By the fourth day I was beginning to feel a little better, with only a cough and still a little fatigued.

The Second Test

After my quarantine was over I felt so much better! I still was not one hundred percent, but definitely better! I was approved by my company's COVID-19 doctor to go back to work since I had not had any fever or coughs within the past three days. I told them that I was not fully recovered, so they decided to give me a few more days of rest, just make sure that I was okay.

After having been quarantined for twenty days, I took another COVID-19 test and guess what? It came back POSITIVE again! I could not believe my ears. The nurse then told me that I would need to go into a second quarantine, and I said "What!!!"

My family was so disappointed and so was I, although I didn't let them know. Now I knew that God had a purpose for these cases, and I continued to put my trust in His word and believe that I was healed.

Overtime Number Two

To get through this, I thought on the game of basketball. At the end of regulation if the game is tied both teams have to play five minutes in overtime. By the end of the five minutes, if the score is still tied, they must play another five minutes until one of the teams is a winner.

God is faithful to His word. If you are in a major challenge in your life right now, just know that God's word is the deciding factor. While being in isolation, I had more time to build my relationship with God. My prayer and meditation time were monumental in hearing His voice with clarity. When the game is in overtime, it's important to listen to the coach (God). Ecclesiastes 9:11 says, "The race is not given to the swift, nor the battle to the strong, but he that endures that endures to the end." It's not to how you start, but how you finish. I eventually tested negative for COVID-19.

Resistance

A body builder becomes strong though resistance. When the weights are heavy, and his muscles seem to get challenged, he pushes against the opposing force and it strengthens his muscles and makes him stronger.

When we resist the devil, it makes us stronger in our faith. God says, "Behold, I give you power over all the powers of the enemy, and nothing by any means, shall hurt you."

God knows everything from the beginning to the end. Hebrews 11 says, "Now faith is the substance of the things hoped for and the evidence of things not seen."

Many times in my basketball career, I did not know what steps to take to qualify for a professional team, but I remembered that the steps of a good man are ordered by the Lord. I trusted Him even when I couldn't see my way. He always makes a way somehow.

You Were Born to Lead

 One day, I was giving a motivational speech for a local school. There were cameras all around filming me as I spoke. Once I finished speaking, I noticed a little girl that had her hand raised. I then motioned for her to ask her question and she asked, "How do you feel about having cameras following you and people pointing at you everywhere that you go?" I answered, "I was born for this." I made an impression on those students that day. I let them know that they have a calling and a gift also and that they were born for a specific purpose.

David, for example was preordained by God to be king. Even though David wasn't his father's choice, he was God's choice. As long as you know you are chosen by God for a particular task there is no force that can stop you; only you can stop yourself.

Pictured: Kelvin's Granddaughters: J'la, Kyla and Nijah

BIOGRAPHY

Kelvin Davis was born on July 12, 1959 in New Brunswick, New Jersey. Kelvin is married and has six beautiful children. Kelvin grew up in a small town called Evergreen, Alabama, where he became a local standout basketball player. He attended high school at Lyeffion High School and graduated in 1977 and went on to attend Jefferson Davis State Junior College in Brewton, Alabama on a basketball scholarship. In 1979, he received a scholarship to Alabama State University. It was there that he obtained a Bachelor of Science degree in 1982. Now Kelvin travels worldwide doing motivational speeches about his amazing story.

Pictured: Kelvin in Ghana with Residents

Made in the USA
Columbia, SC
06 July 2021